GOD'S ARMORBEARER
How To Serve God's Leaders

GOD'S ARMORBEARER
How To Serve God's Leaders

by
Terry Nance

Harrison House
Tulsa, Oklahoma

Unless otherwise indicated, all Scripture quotations are taken from the *King James Version* of the Bible.

Scripture quotations marked *AMP* are taken from *The Amplified Bible, Old Testament.* Copyright © 1962, 1964 by Zondervan Publishing House, Grand Rapids, Michigan.

22nd Printing

GOD'S ARMORBEARER: How To Serve God's Leaders
ISBN 089274-723-4
Copyright © 1990 by Terry Nance
Agape Church
P.O. Box 22007
Little Rock, AR 72221

Published by Harrison House, Inc.
P.O. Box 35035
Tulsa, Oklahoma 74153

Dedication

This book is lovingly dedicated to my mom, Jean Nance, a godly woman of love, prayer and faithfulness.

Special thanks to Mike Camacho for the research material which he provided me on the word *armorbearer*.

Contents

Foreword

He that delicately bringeth up his servant from a child shall have him become his son at the length (Prov. 29:21).

This scripture accurately describes the spiritual relationship between Terry Nance and myself.

As Terry gave himself to God for the fulfilling of his calling, the ministry of a true armorbearer came forth and blossomed.

This book should be required reading for every pastor and every associate in the Body of Christ. It should be used as a textbook in every Bible college and university.

If we will allow the character of Christ to develop within each of us and serve one another, we shall come into the unity of the faith, and of the knowledge of the Son of God, unto a perfect man, unto the measure of the stature of the fullness of Christ.

Happy Caldwell
Agape Church
Little Rock, Arkansas

1

Revelation of an Armorbearer

One evening back in 1983, I felt a prompting to get alone with the Lord. I went into our living room and began to pray. Suddenly I was quickened in my spirit to read the story of David and Saul. I knew the Lord was ready to reveal something to me.

As I began to read, I came to 1 Samuel 16:21:

> **And David came to Saul, and stood before him: and he loved him greatly; and he became his armourbearer.**

Suddenly the Lord quickened the word *armourbearer* to me. He said, "I have called you to be Pastor Caldwell's *armorbearer."*

What does an armorbearer do? In Old Testament days, he was the one responsible for carrying his master's shield into battle. He had the awesome responsibility of seeing to the safety of his officer.

God was getting my priorities in order at that time of my life. It is my prayer that, as you read this book, He will do the same for you.

The Spirit of an Armorbearer

We live in a world that seems to know very little about laying down one's life for another. A full understanding of this concept is vital to the Christian, especially if he knows he has been called into the ministry.

Instead of offering ourselves to wait on others, we in the Church often expect them to wait on us. This is particularly true of our attitude toward the man or woman of God.

You and I will never flow in the anointing of Elisha until we have learned to serve an Elijah. Jesus said, **Greater love hath no man than this, that a man lay down his life for his friends** (John 15:13). It is not difficult to claim that we are submitted to Jesus, but the question is: are we submitted to another human being? That is a different story.

One day I asked God, "What about *my* dreams and desires?" He told me to give them to Him and to work at fulfilling the desires and visions of my pastor, assuring me that if I would do so, He would see to it that my dreams and desires would be fulfilled. He reminded me that that is exactly what Jesus did. He gave up His own will and desire in order to do the Father's will for His life. In turn, the Father made sure that Jesus' dreams and visions were all fulfilled.

The purpose of this book is to give you a revelation of *the spirit of an armorbearer* in your relationship with the man or woman of God in your life.

The Need for Armorbearers

My pastor understands the calling and anointing on my life, and it is his desire to see that calling fulfilled. On the other hand, I understand my God-given duty to stand with my pastor and help him fulfill the vision

God has given both of us, and to fully submit myself to him.

There is a great fear today among many pastors that their associates are out to steal the sheep from them. As a result, there is little or no trust between the pastor and his assistant, no flow between the two of them. I believe God has someone prepared for every pastor (and others of the five-fold ministry), someone to stand with him in the ministry.

I see today great ministries which are built around one person. What will happen when he is gone? It is of no credit to a pastor, or any man of God, to know that when he leaves town the sheep cannot function. The sheep should have their eyes fixed on Jesus, not the pastor. And there should be capable men to run the ministry while the pastor is absent.

Where would we be today if Jesus had not put a portion of Himself into the twelve disciples? What would have happened if, on the day He ascended to the Father, there had been no one there to see Him go and then to take up His ministry on earth?

I ask every pastor and spiritual leader this vital question: If you were taken off the scene today, where would your ministry be tomorrow? Most would have to admit that it would suffer. Jesus' ministry increased and multiplied. That's because there were armorbearers standing with Him.

Definition of the Word *Armorbearer*

The word *armorbearer* is listed eighteen times in Strong's concordance. All of the references are from the Old Testament. Each of these listings is referenced by two numbers, indicating that the word was originally translated from *two* Hebrew words.

Before beginning a study of the actual scriptures in which this word appears, let's consider its original meaning, which must be firmly established if the true idea of the term is to be fully understood.

As we have noted, the *King James* word *armourbearer* was translated from two Hebrew words. The first is *nasa* or *nacah (naw-saw')*. This is a primary word meaning "to *lift.*" It has a great variety of applications, both figuratively and literally. Some of the more interesting applications are to: accept, advance, bear, bear up, carry away, cast, desire, furnish, further, give, help, hold up, lift, pardon, raise, regard, respect, stir up, yield.

The second Hebrew word is *keliy (kel-ee')*, which comes from the root word *kalah (kaw-law')*, meaning "to *end.*" Some of the applications of this root word are to: complete, consume, destroy utterly, be done, finish, fulfill, long, bring to pass, wholly reap, make clean riddance.

From these two Hebrew words, we can see the duty of the armorbearer was to stand beside his leader to assist him, to lift him up, and to protect him against any enemy that might attack him.

Developing the Spirit of an Armorbearer

My purpose in writing this book is not to boast of how humble I have become by serving my pastor, but to help put an end to division in the Body of Christ. Like everyone who reads this book, I too have to deal with the temptation to get into strife, to refuse to submit in some areas of life. But the Lord has given me grace and I have learned to call upon Him and to trust Him completely to direct my steps.

You too can be set free from rebellion, strife and contention when you develop the spirit of an armorbearer.

Even though this book is written from the viewpoint and position of an associate minister, please do not think that it does not relate to you. It will help anyone who is a part of the Body of Christ, anyone who desires to fulfill his or her God-given call. To the person in the five-fold ministry, I say this: You will never arrive at a place where you do not have to submit to anyone. The spirit of an armorbearer is the spirit of Christ. It is the heart of a servant.

Now let's take a look into the function of an armorbearer.

2
Function of an Armorbearer

As we look at the function of an armorbearer, I would like for you to allow the Holy Spirit to quicken your heart and reveal to you where you may have failed to flow with your spiritual leaders. Make a quality decision to rid yourself of any trace of rebellion, strife, contention, competitiveness and unforgiveness; determining to faithfully fulfill your rightful place in the Body of Christ.

The main function of one who is designated as an armorbearer is that of service; he is to help and assist another. Let's look at some of the different forms this service takes.

Duties of an Armorbearer

An armorbearer...

1. Must provide strength for his leader.

By his very presence, a true armorbearer will always display and produce an attitude of faith and peace.

If you are to be successful in service as an armorbearer to your pastor, he must sense the joy and victory which is an integral part of your lifestyle. That alone will minister to him. It is a great relief to the pastor to know that he does not have to carry his assistant physically, mentally and spiritually. Many times I have seen pastors drained physically and emotionally because their associate was always in need of something. Your pastor has plenty of sheep to take care of; he doesn't need another. You should be assisting him, giving him much-needed rest in mind and body by demonstrating that your faith is strong and active.

2. Must have a deep-down sense of respect for his leader, and acceptance for, and tolerance of, his leader's personality and his way of doing things.

God made us all different. At least fifty percent of the time, your pastor's way of doing things will differ from yours. That difference should not be allowed to cause a problem for you or your spiritual leader.

Several years ago, I learned a secret which has helped me to flow in harmony with my pastor. I determined that if the end result of my pastor's plan is to build and extend the Kingdom of God and win souls for Jesus, then I am willing to flow with the plan. Our goal is the same, our methods different. But what does it really matter whose methods are used, as long as the goal is reached?

If you will adopt this attitude toward your pastor, there will be a knitting of hearts between the two of you. He will know that you are not there to argue with him or to challenge his decisions, but that you are there to work with him in achieving his God-given objectives.

3. Must instinctively understand his leader's thoughts.

I can hear what you are probably thinking right now: "My pastor and I just don't think alike." That's right; no two people do. And that is one of the problems which must be dealt with in being an armorbearer to another.

Instead of complaining about your differences, begin to discover and confess your agreement: "In Jesus' name, I understand how my pastor thinks and I flow with him in the spirit of understanding."

Remember, the disciples were with Jesus for three long years and yet they did not begin to think as He thought until after He had died, been buried and resurrected, ascended into heaven and sent the Holy Ghost. Just as God's Spirit was eventually imparted to these men, after a period of time your pastor's spirit will come upon you, and you two will become like-minded.

4. Must walk in agreement with and submission to his leader.

In order to be an armorbearer, you must have it settled in your heart that according to Romans 13:1,2, all authority is ordained of God. You must make up your mind to submit to your pastor in the same way that you would submit to Jesus.

Most Christians do not understand the true meaning of submission to authority. The Bible teaches that all authority has been instituted by God Himself, so to refuse to submit to God's delegated authority is to refuse to submit to God.

"Oh, but I will always submit myself to God!"

This is a comment I hear quite often. But how can a person claim to be submitted to God if he or she refuses to submit to God's delegated authority?

We must not look at the person, but at the office he occupies. We do not regard the man, but the position. We obey, not the individual himself, but God's authority in him. Anything less than full submission is rebellion, and rebellion is the principle on which Satan and his kingdom operate.

It is sad to think that we Christians can preach the truth with our lips, but go right on living by a satanic principle in our everyday lives. How can we expect to preach the Gospel to others and to bring them under God's authority if we ourselves have not yet fully submitted to that authority?

There is a spirit of independence at large in the Body of Christ today. Independent churches produce independent spirits. We must break this spirit and begin to rightly discern the whole Body of Christ.

The Apostle Peter tells us: **Likewise, ye younger, submit yourselves unto the elders...**(1 Pet. 5:5). There are no conditions to this command, except in the case of an elder who is giving directives which are in direct violation of the scriptures. Then the individual believer must obey a higher authority, which is God's Word.

Always remember this: God will never establish you as an authority until you have first learned to submit to authority.

5. Must make the advancement of his leader his most important goal.

When I asked the Lord, "What about *my* dreams and goals, the vision You have placed in *my* heart?" He said to me: "Son, you are not to live for the fulfillment of your dreams or vision. Set it as your goal to achieve your pastor's dreams, and I will make sure that yours are fulfilled."

I can honestly say that God has done that very thing in my life. Twelve years ago I had a vision to reach out into many nations. In 1982, I began to see that vision come to pass. I have already traveled to over twenty countries, and have preached in most of them. We are now establishing churches and Bible schools in five of those nations. All this has come about because I decided to do what Jesus did; He sacrificed His own desires in order to fulfill the Father's will. If you will do the same thing, God will exalt you, no matter what circumstances you may face.

6. *Must possess endless strength so as to thrust, press and force his way onward without giving way under harsh treatment.*

> **For what glory is it, if, when ye be buffeted for your faults, ye shall take it patiently? but if, when ye do well, and suffer for it, ye take it patiently, this is acceptable with God.**
>
> **1 Peter 2:20**

This passage makes it very clear that there will be times in the midst of battle when you and I will feel that we are being wrongfully treated. These types of situations are bound to arise, but do not allow Satan to put resentment into your heart. Learn to give the situation over to the Lord and endure what comes patiently; God will be pleased with you.

It may be that in your heart you know you made the right decision. But in the eyes of your leader, it may seem wrong. Such times will develop character in you, if you will walk in love, allowing the Spirit of God to take charge of the matter. Your strength will always come by encouraging yourself in the Lord, as David did in 1 Samuel 30:6.

The easy thing to do is quit, saying, "Well, no one around here appreciates me; I was rebuked and I know I was right in what I did." Do not give into the flesh.

Get in prayer and stay there until 1 Peter 2:20 has become a part of your very being. Victory will spring forth and you will say with David of old, "I will bless the Lord at all times." (Ps. 34:1.)

7. Must follow orders immediately and correctly.

In order to be a good leader, one must be a good follower. And being a good follower means taking care of things quickly and efficiently. If you aspire to become a leader, then the one you serve today must be able to depend upon you to carry out his directives. Here are some simple keys to help you to become a better follower so that some day you may be a better leader:

First, write everything down. I know what you're probably thinking: "Boy, what a revelation!" But let's be practical. God had everything written down for us so we would not forget anything. We dare not do any less for ourselves. Write down the orders of your leader just as a waiter writes down an order for food. Make sure your leader gets exactly *what he ordered.*

Second, ask your leader to explain anything you don't understand. Make sure you have the correct information before you leave to carry out the order. Many times we misrepresent our leader because we misunderstand what he means.

Third, treat your orders as highest priority. When asked to do something, do it immediately! I am always blessed when my secretary is efficient. Her efficiency ministers to me. The same results will come when you put your heart into carrying out instructions quickly and correctly.

8. Must be a support to his leader.

Every pastor needs a group of faithful supporters, especially among his associates and staff. The word supporter means "that which supports or upholds; a sustainer; a comforter; a maintainer; a defender."

Contrary to popular belief, pastors are human just like anyone else. They hurt; they make mistakes; they get frustrated and bothered; many times they face discouragement and disappointment. As armorbearers, our job is to uphold, sustain, maintain and defend our leader, being there for him to lean on in times of need.

Right now, as I am writing this, I am laughing because I can just hear the voice of some staff member or associate crying out: "What about *me?* What about *my* hurts, wounds and problems?" I will be honest with you. We have too many babies in the Body of Christ. It's time we started laying down our lives for someone else, putting our trust in God to take care of our hurts and frustrations.

There are many associates whose only desire and goal is to stand up in front of people and preach. They want to be in front of the pastor — until war breaks out; then they suddenly jump behind him! God has called you and me to go out in front of our pastor for only one reason, and that is to raise up our shield of faith and protect him from the harmful words of people and the fiery darts of the devil.

You will never make any real progress toward leadership until you have first mastered the art of supporting your spiritual leader.

9. Must be an excellent communicator.

Communication is more important than anything I know of in establishing a relationship with a leader.

It is the only way to build trust between the pastor and his associates. This does not mean that you are to bother your pastor with every issue or decision that comes up; just that you should let him be aware of what is going on in the church and among the people.

In my years of service as an associate minister, I have learned a very valuable lesson: *Never hide anything from your pastor.* Always let him know if someone is having (or causing) a problem in the church, and what steps you are taking to resolve that situation.

Many times I have to deal with things which I know are clearly in my area of responsibility, but I always make my pastor aware of what I am doing. Situations will sometimes arise which I know should be dealt with by the pastor himself. When that happens, I go and share with him. Either he will deal with the situation, or he will give me advice as to how to handle it.

The "bottom line" is communication.

If anyone ever says to you, "I want to tell you something in private, but you must promise not to let the pastor know I told you about it," you should stop that conversation immediately and say to the person, "You may as well hold your breath, because I will not make any such promise."

You owe it to your leader to reveal anything that is going to cause problems in the church. Jesus said that there is nothing hidden that will not be revealed. (Mark 4:22.) If you withhold something from your pastor, then I can safely prophesy that it will come back to you; it will blow up and you will be caught in the middle of the explosion.

Secrecy is a trap which Satan lays for the unsuspecting. Don't fall into it.

10. Must have a disposition that will eagerly gain victories for his leader.

In 2 Samuel 22:36 David said of the Lord, **...thy gentleness hath made me great.** David was a great warrior, but he declared that it wasn't his boldness, assurance or strength that made him great; rather, it was God's gentleness. This is the character trait that will gain victories for the leader and the one who serves him as armorbearer.

Armed with this attitude, you will represent your leader well and gain much favor. Always remember that as an associate or assistant, wherever you go and whatever you do, you represent your pastor. You do not want to do anything to bring a reproach to him or the church you both serve.

I have seen times when the pastor has asked an associate to make some changes throughout his department. The associate then calls his staff together and tells them: "Pastor has said that you had better straighten up or out you go." That makes a pastor look as if he is some kind of unholy, ruthless king sitting on his throne barking out orders.

This kind of thing happens all the time in churches, and the result is always strife. The only reason any associate would say such a thing is to make it look as if he really cares for the people under him, but the pastor doesn't. It is just an attempt to save his own reputation at the expense of the pastor's. A true armorbearer will always strive to represent his pastor well before all men.

When we work with people, we face many delicate situations every day. Even though you are not the shepherd of the flock, as an associate you must take into your spirit the heart of a shepherd. You must learn to deal with people in love and find some common ground of agreement with the ones with whom you work and deal. No one is unreachable as long as he is teachable.

In my fifteen years of experience as an associate, I have sat with people and explained to them what my pastor meant by a statement he has made. Some people are easily offended, and many times they will come to the associate before going directly to the pastor. When people come to me in such situations, I try to help them understand what my pastor really meant because I know his heart. From there, I encourage them to make an appointment to meet with him personally to discuss the matter.

I encourage you to trust God every day for a spirit of *humility, meekness, forgiveness, purity* and a *clear conscience.* These virtues will keep a guard around you, and then what an asset you will be to the ministry.

11. Must have the ability to minister strength and courage to his leader.

In order to minister strength and courage, an armorbearer must possess an endless fountain of these virtues himself. The word *courage* means "bravery; the ability to encounter difficulties and danger with firmness, boldness and valor."

When your pastor stands up and says, "Thus saith the Lord, 'Build the church building without going into debt,' " what is your reaction?

Some may say, "The pastor is really missing it this time."

How do you respond?

Remember when the children of Israel were told to go into the Promised Land and overcome it? (Numbers 13.) They sent twelve spies into the land who came back and reported on what they had seen there. Only two of the twelve had the courage to say, "Let's go up and take it, for we are well able to do so." (v. 30.) Everyone else said, "No, we can't do it."

Whenever God speaks to your Moses, then be like Joshua and Caleb, the two strong, courageous spies. Stand up in faith and courage and go forth to take the land — no matter how big the task may be.

In Numbers 14:4 we read this about the faithless, fearful children of Israel: **And they said one to another, Let us make a captain, and let us return into Egypt.** Many times the first choice of a new captain will be the associate minister. When a portion of the people begin to call out for you to become their new leader — beware. When they are ready to make you captain in place of the pastor, because you will lead them the way they want to go — look out! That is a deception and temptation from Satan. That is not the way to success and life, it is the way into sin and rebellion. God is never in such a movement.

Courage comes from faith in God. In order to minister the same assurance your pastor has, you must stay built up in the Word of God. This edification comes only by putting the Word first.

Another deception and temptation from Satan which must be guarded against and overcome is the false idea that the pastor is more concerned with fulfilling his own personal vision than he is with meeting the needs of his associates and staff members. The lie is that the pastor will go to any limits to accomplish his own goal, but will not go out of his way to help meet the goals of those who work with him.

Remember one thing: the vision of the church you are called to serve is God's vision, and if He did not think you could fit in with it, He would never have placed you in that ministry to begin with. You will not always get a pat on the back for doing a good job. As Christians, our rewards are waiting for us in heaven. Would you prefer for your pastor to pat you on the back and say, "Good job," or for Jesus to pat you on the back and say, "Well done, good and faithful servant"?

God is a wonderful accountant, and some day the books will be opened and the rewards distributed. I trust that your rewards will be great. They will be determined by your attitude here and now on this earth.

Functions of an Armorbearer

Now let's look at some other functions of the armorbearer in order to get a better understanding of the loyalty and the attitude of heart which must be developed to fulfill this divine calling.

The true armorbearer:

_____ Awakens and arouses his leader, helping him to stand against all foes.

_____ Carries and handles his leader's weapons resourcefully.

_____ Moves quickly alongside his leader through the thick of battle as a forceful escort who never falls behind.

_____ Protects and watches out for his leader continually and continuously.

_____ Repels any type of attack against his leader.

_____ Rescues his leader from all difficulties and hardships.

_____ Moves to resist totally and completely every enemy advance which comes against his leader to do him harm.

_____ Opposes and routs his leader's enemies swiftly and forcefully.

_____ Remains always on duty at his leader's side to tend to any need which may arise.

_____ Keeps one eye on the leader at all times and the other eye trained on the enemy, anticipating the actions of both.

_____ Surrenders completely to his leader, trusting him implicitly and obeying without hesitation his every command.

_____ Carries out every plan of his leader successfully.

_____ Completes his leader's commands perfectly.

_____ Assists his leader in all activities and undertakings.

_____ Organizes and arranges his leader's activities.

_____ Prepares and cares for his leader's belongings.

_____ Takes very special care in the selection and preparation of his leader's supplies.

_____ Anticipates his leader's needs and demands so as to properly furnish and supply what is needed.

_____ Keeps his eye on the road ahead so as to point out to his leader any danger or pitfall.

_____ Recognizes and brings to his leader's attention any questionable matters or any vital information.

_____ Strives to make his leader's surroundings more pleasant and bearable.

_____ Develops an eye for detail.

_____ Helps bring an acceleration in growth and promotion to his leader's progress.

_____ Places primary emphasis on enhancing the leader's position, guarding against any personal jealousy, envy or selfishness.

_____ Exalts, respects and uplifts his leader at all times.

_____ Watches for his officer's every reward, claiming those which the leader may have overlooked.

_____ Works tirelessly and diligently on behalf of his leader, seeking ways to advance his welfare and situation.

_____ Fulfills his leader in every way, getting along with him, and making him feel comfortable in giving orders.

_____ Sacrifices his own life and well-being for the betterment of his leader.

_____ Works for his leader's welfare at all time.

_____ Demonstrates total intolerance of any false charge made against his leader.

_____ Shares the dreams, goals and visions of his leader.

_____ Desires to see his leader "get ahead."

_____ Forgives his leader for any offense immediately and without harboring resentment or anger.

_____ Refuses to hold a grudge against his leader for any reason.

_____Demonstrates extreme loyalty to his leader, even unto death.

_____ Completes and complements his leader.

_____ Flows well with his leader.

_____ Esteems his leader as more important than himself.

It is obvious by now that a biblical armorbearer was much more than just a hired hand. An armorbearer was a person who undoubtedly spent many years, if not his entire life, in his officer's service. Only in this manner could he come to know and understand his officer.

Servant, bodyguard, friend, companion, butler, cook and confidant are just some of the many roles the armorbearer filled in the life of his officer. His list of duties was interminable. The position of armorbearer is one which requires great honor, love, tolerance and watchfulness. Unquestioning obedience was absolutely necessary, although after a few years of service the faithful armorbearer probably did not need to be told what his officer thought, desired or required. He knew him as he knew himself.

Dedication and devotion unto death was the order of each day for the biblical armorbearer.

Although there is no reference material available to indicate the exact procedure involved in the selection and training of an armorbearer in biblical days, it seems clear that whatever method was used, it was obviously a position of heartfelt loyalty. It is also evident that the armorbearer was chosen and trained by the officer he would serve.

In Chapter 5 we will consider some of the qualifications for this vital position of spiritual armorbearer.

3

Armorbearers of the Old Testament

A good example of the loyalty of an armorbearer is found in the story of the death of Abimelech. (Judges 9:45-55.)

This event took place during a war in which Abimelech was laying siege to a city. He was succeeding in his attempt to seize the city and had the enemy on the run. When he came to a tower where many of the people had taken refuge, he was prepared to burn it down. As wood was being laid at the foot of the tower, a woman in the top threw down a piece of millstone which struck Abimelech on the head, cracking his skull. He went to his armorbearer and ordered the young man, **...Draw thy sword, and slay me, that men say not of me, A woman slew him...**(v. 54).

Even though Abimelech was wicked, the loyalty of his armorbearer is obvious. He was the closest person to the king when the stone struck him on the head. He was just as concerned about Abimelech's tainted honor as Abimelech was himself. He did not want it said that his officer had been killed by a woman. His instant obedience is also recorded: **...And his young man thrust him through, and he died** (v. 54).

Saul's Armorbearer

In 1 Samuel 31:4-6 and 1 Chronicles 10:4,5, we find another account of an officer at war, his armorbearer at his side. Saul and his army were fighting against the Philistines and were losing ground. Saul's army, realizing that defeat was imminent, turned to flee. His men, including his sons, were killed and Saul was wounded by arrows. He turned to his armorbearer and ordered him: **...Draw thy sword, and thrust me though therewith; lest these uncircumcised come and thrust me through, and abuse me...**(1 Sam. 31:4).

Saul wanted to die at the hands of his armorbearer rather than be captured and tortured by the enemy. However, his armorbearer would not oblige him, so Saul took his own life by falling on his sword. **And when his armourbearer saw that Saul was dead, he fell likewise upon his sword, and died with him** (v. 5).

There are many things revealed in this portion of scripture.

At some point in the battle, Saul's forces turned to flee. His army was put to rout, his men killed. Later on in the chase, his three sons were slain. The enemy came close enough to wound Saul. That was when he turned to his armorbearer and made his request to die at his hands.

Note that although everyone else had fled, leaving Saul to face the whole enemy army alone, his faithful armorbearer was right alongside of him. Saul, being the king, rode on the back of the fastest horse or in the swiftest chariot. If he traveled by chariot, then his armorbearer was his driver. If he went on horseback, then Saul's horse must have been chosen by his armorbearer because it was part of his duty to select and care for his officer's mount, equipment and supplies. Needless to say, the armorbearer's horse had to be of equal strength, speed and stamina as his master's.

The armorbearer could be trusted to choose and select for his officer because he knew how his commander thought and what he liked and needed.

Through all the fighting and fleeing, Saul's armorbearer had managed to dodge the arrows and stay right alongside his leader. When Saul commanded his faithful servant to thrust him through with his sword, **...his armourbearer would not; for he was sore afraid...**(v. 4).

It seems peculiar that an armorbearer would be "sore afraid." He had been selected, trained and prepared to serve in battle. Because he was an armorbearer to the king, he was probably more skilled in warfare than any other soldier in the king's army. His duty was to protect the commander-in-chief. It doesn't seem logical that a man who was trained and prepared to give his life to save and defend the king would be afraid.

In the Hebrew, this word translated afraid in the *King James Version* is *yare'* *(yaw-ray')*. It does not mean to fear in the sense of being frightened or terrorized, but to fear out of *reverence!* In this case, it means "to *sorely respect and honor"!*

Now the armorbearer's reaction is much more understandable.

This man had spent all his time in Saul's service, caring for and protecting him. His entire reason for being was the preservation of the life of the king. If there was even the slightest chance that Saul could be saved from destruction, then he had to take that chance, regardless of the odds against its success.

Perhaps it was just too much to ask the man who had protected Saul all this time to take the very life he was pledged to defend. He just could not bring himself to destroy the one he had spent his life preserving and protecting.

Two Different Armorbearers

Notice the reaction of Saul's armorbearer as contrasted with that of Abimelech's servant, who did kill his officer when ordered to do so. Here we see two different reactions from men both of whom had dedicated and sacrificed their lives to the welfare of their superiors. Perhaps the reason their reactions were different is because the circumstances were different.

Although Saul had been severely wounded by arrows, perhaps his armorbearer did not judge his wounds to be fatal. The young man was probably trained in attending to battle wounds. Perhaps he would have preferred to try to outrun the Philistines and hide somewhere, so he could nurse Saul back to health.

Abimelech had been hit on the head with a large piece of millstone, and his skull had been crushed. The wound was probably not very pretty. Perhaps the contents of his skull were coming out of the wound. Death seemed inevitable.

Saul said, "Draw your sword and thrust me through, lest these uncircumcised come and thrust me through and abuse me."

36

Abimelech said, "Draw your sword and kill me, so people won't say that I was killed by a woman."

The difference is that Abimelech was dying; Saul was not. Saul simply feared that the Philistines would come and torture him.

Perhaps Saul's armorbearer would rather have tried to escape with his commander, or maybe even to fight to the death alongside him. But one thing is for sure: out of *respect*, he could not be the one to put an end to Saul's life. It was a sense of reverential fear, respect and honor, not "fright" that caused the armorbearer to fail to obey his king.

When Saul realized that his armorbearer would not comply with his request, he fell on his own sword. In true armorbearer fashion, as a man who had spent his whole life following Saul, the armorbearer knew that this was no time to stop now. When his master fell on his own sword and ended his life, the armorbearer had no more reason to live. Out of respect for his officer, he also fell on his sword. Suicide had not been his idea. In fact, if Saul had asked, his armorbearer may have even had a better strategy or a plan to escape from the hands of the Philistines. But since Saul chose to end his life, so did his faithful servant.

Jonathan's Armorbearer

In 1 Samuel 14:1-23 there is another account of a relationship between a young man and his armorbearer. Jonathan ordered his armorbearer to accompany him over to the garrison of the Philistines against whom he and the other Israelites were warring. He wanted to go over single-handed. Jonathan had not told his father, Saul, of his intentions. Though the king knew nothing about the plan, and though he and his master were only two against an entire army, Jonathan's armorbearer obeyed.

In verse 6, Jonathan says: **...Come, and let us go over unto the garrison of these uncircumcised: it may be that the Lord will work for us: for there is no restraint to the Lord to save by many or by few.** In verse 7, the young and fearless armorbearer answers: **...Do all that is in thine heart: turn thee; behold, I am with thee according to thy heart.**

As the two young men climbed up toward the enemy's camp, God confirmed to them that He had, in fact, delivered the enemy into their hand. Jonathan turned to his companion and said, **...Come up after me...**(v. 12).

When they reached the place where the enemy was standing, **....they fell before Jonathan; and his armourbearer slew after him** (v. 13.) Then the passage goes on to explain how God saved the whole nation of Israel that day, through the brave actions of Jonathan and his faithful, obedient armorbearer.

It is curious to note that Jonathan said, "It *may* be that the Lord will work for us." Although Jonathan was not certain about what would happen, his armorbearer was more than willing to follow. Verse 7 reveals his answer, and the proper attitude of any armorbearer:

> ..."Do all that is in your heart. Go then; here I am with you, according to your heart."
> **New King James Version**

> ...Do all that is in your mind; I am with you in whatever you think [best].
> **The Amplified Bible**

"Do all that you have in mind....Go ahead; I am
with you heart and soul."
New International Version

..."Whatever you want to do, I am with you."
Good News Version

"Fine!....Do as you think best; I'm with you heart
and soul, whatever you decide."
The Living Bible

As they approached the enemy, Jonathan's
armorbearer knew his place. He was to come *after*
Jonathan.

In verse 13 we see that it was the anointing upon
Jonathan, the anointing of a leader, that caused the
enemy to fall. The young armorbearer was diligent to
follow along *after* his officer, destroying the enemy who
had been knocked to the ground by God's anointing
upon his leader: "...and his armourbearer slew after
him." (v. 13.)

This is a classic example of the humility and
diligence of a biblical armorbearer. He is one who wins
victories and slays enemies while his leader gets the
glory...one who trusts his officer, even in what may
appear to be a whim...one who takes his place *behind*
the man he serves, not striving to get out in front.

David as Armorbearer

In 1 Samuel 16:14-23 we find the story of the last
of the five armorbearers.

King Saul was troubled. He had a distressing
spirit. He decided to find a skillful musician who could
ease his state of mind when he was oppressed. A young
man was recommended to the king by one of his
servants:

> ...Behold, I have seen a son of Jesse the Bethlehemite, that is cunning in playing, and a mighty valiant man, and a man of war, and prudent in matters, and a comely person, and the Lord is with him.
>
> 1 Samuel 16:18

The young man was sent to Saul, bearing gifts. We are told that Saul "loved him greatly" and made him his armorbearer. (v. 21.) He could minister strength to Saul, causing him to feel "refreshed" and "well." (v. 23.)

In verse 18 we see that the young armorbearer was described as:

1. Skillful in playing

2. A mighty man of valor

3. A man of war

4. Prudent in speech

5. Handsome in appearance

6. One whom the Lord was with

All of these qualities are biblical descriptions of a true armorbearer.

Perhaps the fact that David had once been Saul's armorbearer further explains his attitude when he later declared that he would not touch "the Lord's anointed." (1 Sam. 26:9.) No matter how hard Saul tried to kill David, and no matter how many opportunities David had to slay Saul, David never struck back.

Did David walk in the same fear that caused Saul's future armorbearer to refuse to kill him? More than likely. This respect and honor toward God's anointed may also explain David's attitude of extreme repentance, sorrow and humility before Saul after he had sneaked up behind the king in a cave and cut off the edge of his robe. (1 Sam. 24:1-6.)

David was a true armorbearer, one who held no grudges but who faithfully and obediently withstood his captain's harsh treatment. The result was his own eventual promotion to a place of high respect and honor.

4
New Testament Armorbearing

Thus far we have investigated the Old Testament concerning the subject of armorbearing, and we have clearly defined the duty, role and service of the armorbearer in his Old Testament function. Now let's look more closely at this role of armorbearing in the light of the New Testament.

The Ministry of Armorbearing

In the life of every Christian, God has established a certain order of priorities. Both the armorbearer and the person he is serving should follow these priorities, if they are to live faithful Christian lives. In descending order of importance, these priorities are:

1. Relationship with God
2. Relationship with spouse
3. Relationship with children
4. Employment or work

One of the main differences between armorbearing in the Old Testament and in the New Testament is the fact that in Old Testament days the duty of an armorbearer was priority number one. In the New Testament, armorbearing is priority number four. This doesn't mean that today's armorbearer is to take less than necessary care of his responsibility. His position is a God-given one, and he must be a good steward of that duty. Although the physical roles may have changed, the attitude of the heart must be the same.

The position of armorbearer is not likely to be one to which God would call a person for only a short period of time; rather, it remains a position of devotion and heartfelt loyalty.

In comparing this office to the office of an associate or any position of the ministry, the individual must realize that God has not called him to use that position as a stepping stone. We have seen this happen so many times in the Body of Christ, and it is a reproach to God.

If a person feels that the only reason God has him where he is now is so he can be promoted to "something bigger and better," then it's sad to say but that individual is operating in the world's system. This type of individual says, "Whoever offers me the most money or authority gets my services."

Did you ever stop and ask God if your current position is the one He has chosen for you, if where you are now is where He wants you to be? It makes no difference what the salary or working conditions are like; what really matters is, has God called you to that job and place?

While serving my pastor, I have had two opportunities to become the pastor of another church. Both of these were good churches, and at the time of the offers the pay would have been better than what I was receiving where I am. Besides all that, I could have been the pastor, rather than an associate. If I had operated by the world's system, I would have jumped at the "chance for advancement." But the Kingdom of God does not operate that way.

I know that I am in God's *divinely appointed* position for me. That is how I pray for the people who come to join the staff in our church. I say, "Lord, send us the people who are divinely appointed by You to be here and work with us."

Unless your people are divinely *called* and *sent* to you by the Lord, you do not want them. I understand that there will be times when God will separate a person from his current position. That moment may come for you one day. But if it does come, you and your pastor will know in the spirit that it is time for a change, and that the separation will be best for all concerned, expecially the Kingdom of God.

On my office wall there hangs a plaque which reads: "Bloom where you are planted." I believe and practice that principle, which is based on God's Word. My life is a testimony that the Word of God works.

As armorbearers we must prove ourselves faithful where God has "planted" us. Let God exalt and promote you where you are. If you will be diligent, faithful, humble and motivated by the heart of a servant, you will find the principles of God's Word working for you.

The Bible tells us, "Humble yourself before God, and He will exalt you." (1 Pet. 5:6.) I know in my heart that if God ever says it's time for me to leave this position and move on to another, the pastor and I will both know it.

Faithful Armorbearing

I would like to share an interesting story with you as an illustration of faithful armorbearing. Some time ago my pastor, Happy Caldwell of Agape Church in Little Rock, Arkansas, met with the Billy Graham Crusade team which was planning a series of meetings in our city. The crusade coordinator began his talk by stating that he had been with Billy Graham the least amount of time of any of the ministers on the staff.

"I have only been with Billy for 23 *years*," he said.

When I heard that, I was shocked. In charismatic circles we preach faithfulness and staying with something, but the Billy Graham Crusade team lives it. Some staff members and ministers are ready to give up and go on to their reward if God doesn't open up something new and better for them every year. We have got to start seeing our position as one called and instituted of God. We must be willing to stay in it for the rest of our lives, if that is what God wants.

Recently I got on my face before God and prayed, "Lord, if it is Your desire that I stay here as my pastor's armorbearer and serve this ministry in that capacity for the rest of my life, then Your will be done."

Friend, it is no fun to be out of the will of God. We in the Church no longer have the time to be operating outside of the will and plan of our heavenly Father.

If you are an associate or staff minister, I want to encourage you to remain faithful, no matter what pressure you may be facing. I will honestly admit that there have been times when I have wanted to throw in the towel and say to God, "This is too hard; this is not fair."

One day Jesus spoke to me and told me that He was simply asking me to do the same thing He had done on the earth. Jesus fulfilled His Father's desire, and not His own. He is not asking you and me to do anything He Himself has not already done.

At this moment in my life, I am doing more than I have ever done for God. At thirty-three years of age, I travel overseas and do things that I have always dreamed of. I believe it is because I have stayed where God put me.

One day a man came into my office, which is really nice with a beautiful view of a small mountain right behind my desk.

"Well," he said, as he walked in, "how does it feel to be a big man with a huge desk, leather chairs and a view like you've got there?"

Thank the Lord I was in a good mood when he said that. People have no idea what it has taken to get to that place. Any staff minister can relate to my feelings.

If you are not a staff member, I will tell you how it feels. It feels exactly the same way it felt in 1979 when I had an office with a pea-green carpet, an army surplus desk and a small window with a view of the back of a drug store. Did I complain? Heavens, no! Pastor Caldwell had a door laid over two small filing cabinets for a desk. I was jumping up and down with excitement just to be able to say to someone, "Come into my office." It was ugly, but it was *my* office, the first real one I had ever had. I had "birthed" it in the spirit in prayer, and I was as happy and proud of it as I could be.

The Spirit of God may be ministering to you right now because you are at the place of giving up in your ministry. Please don't! Get in the Word and start rejoicing in what you have been blessed with. Put your future into God's hands. Remember, David was faithful to Saul, and look how God exalted him.

One day I walked into my office with everything in the world coming against me. I was discouraged. I felt left out. It seemed that God was going to just have to move me on. At that time, I looked at the Bible on my desk and I cried out to God, saying, "I need help!" I picked up the Bible and it fell open to Ephesians 5. I know God divinely directed me to that chapter. I began to read, and then I came to Ephesians 5:17-19:

> ...be ye not unwise, but understanding what the will of the Lord is.
>
> And be not drunk with wine, wherein is excess; but be filled with the Spirit;
>
> Speaking to yourselves in psalms and hymns and spiritual songs, singing and *making* melody in your heart to the Lord.

As I read that passage, the Lord quickened the word *making* to me. "Son," He said, "a piano makes beautiful music only when someone sits down and plays it."

"The joy, peace, and assurance you need is there," He went on to say, "but you have to make the melody come forth. Get up and start dancing before Me."

I did not want to do that, nor did I feel like it, but I did it in faith. I closed my office door and started to leap and jump for joy, praising God. As I did so, the anointing broke the yoke of oppression.

If you are under a spirit of oppression, then before you read any further in this chapter, get up and start rejoicing. You are set free in Jesus' name. This is God's will for you right now.

Now what about our personal relationship with our officer? In 2 Corinthians 5:16 the Apostle Paul says: **Wherefore, henceforth know we no man after the flesh....** As an armorbearer, you have a called ministry to serve a general of God's army. The Old Testament suggests a very close physical relationship between the officer and his armorbearer. This may be the case in the New Testament, but such a close personal relationship is not necessary to successfully carry out the responsibility of the armorbearer. God did not call you to be your leader's fishing buddy. I am not called to be my pastor's best friend. We are friends, but that is not our primary relationship.

We should never assume a personal right to know or be a part of our officer's family or private life:

> **Be not forward [self-assertive and boastfully ambitious] in the presence of the king, and stand not in the place of great men;**
>
> **For better it is that it be said to you, Come up here, than that you should be put lower in the presence of the prince whose eyes have seen you.**
> **Proverbs 25:6,7 AMP**

I will say this, that a personal relationship of some kind is inevitable, but the armorbearer's primary role is not that of personal friend. The armorbearer's main purpose is to pull down Satan's strongholds for his pastor, church and city. Do not get your feelings hurt if you are not asked to have dinner with the pastor every Friday night. Your goal is not to get next to the pastor, but to get next to Jesus and to do battle in the Spirit.

The Service of an Armorbearer

In the Old Testament, the armorbearer's main function was directly related to combat. This has not changed at all between the Old and New Testaments. What has changed greatly is the type of combat in which the New Testament armorbearer is to engage as he serves his officer:

> **For we wrestle not against flesh and blood, but against principalities, against powers, against the rulers of the darkness of this world, against spiritual wickedness in high places.**
>
> **Ephesians 6:12**

In this passage we clearly see that we are not engaged in battle against the Philistines — against flesh and blood — but against demonic powers.

God calls men and women to do great things and to accomplish wondrous tasks for Him. Preaching the Word of God to all nations is no small undertaking. It is impossible for one person to accomplish it alone. That's where the Body of Christ comes in. God will place *His* vision inside a person, and *His* anointing upon him to carry it forth. Then He will surround that individual with other people who will support and work with him toward the fulfillment of that vision. The Lord will begin by sending God-called ministers to assist the man of God and to take his spirit upon them. These people act as armorbearers; their function is to take the load off their officer, and to help impart his vision to the people.

I have heard preachers refer to the associate ministry as "playing second fiddle." I have a few questions that I would like to ask those who think that way: Did Joshua play second fiddle to Moses? Did

Elisha play second fiddle to Elijah? Does a person's nose play second fiddle to his eyes? Does his foot play second fiddle to his hand?

If you have thought of the associate ministry in this way, I hope that by now your thinking has begun to change.

There is no second fiddle position in the Body of Christ.

> **And those members of the body, which we think to be less honourable, upon these we bestow more abundant honour; and our uncomely parts have more abundant comeliness.**
>
> **1 Corinthians 12:23**

If anyone thinks that because he fills the position of pastor, prophet, apostle, evangelist or teacher he is better than the rest of the Body, then he had better prepare to be brought low, for that is pride, and destruction is waiting for him right around the corner. I trust that you never fall for that kind of deceptive thinking.

God-called armorbearers are there to support the leader and to help fulfill the vision God has given him.

There came a day in my life when I told my pastor that I was behind him. He stopped and said, "No, you are standing with me."

That did not happen overnight, but no relationship is built overnight. Your position in the ministry is important to God, and if you are faithful and patient, you will be exalted in due season.

Deuteronomy 32:30 says that one shall put a thousand to flight, and two will chase ten thousand. See, with you by his side, your officer is ten times more powerful than he is alone.

The Duties of the Armorbearer

We can see that the most important part of the armorbearer's duties lie in the spirit realm. Armorbearing is a ministry of prayer, watchfulness, and intercession. The armorbearer is to prove his sincerity, loyalty, and courage in the spirit realm through prayer and intercession. All the physical tasks of an Old Testament armorbearer apply today, in the spirit. From what we have learned from the Old Testament, based on what we see in the New Testament scriptures, we are able to identify the duties of a New Testament armorbearer.

A true armorbearer:

_____ Strives to keep his godly priorities in line.

_____ Resists seeking to know his leader after the flesh.

_____ Remains always humble, with fear and trembling, in sincerity of heart, doing what is pleasing to Christ, "not with eyeservice as menpleasers."

_____ Serves his leader well, expecting no reward from man, but knowing that Jesus will reward him one day for his efforts and loyalty.

_____ Aids his leader in spiritual combat.

_____ Ministers strength to his leader in the spirit.

_____ Helps his leader to stand against the wiles of the devil.

_____ Knows how to deal with spiritual forces.

Even though the word *armorbearer* is not used in the New Testament, we can see from the scriptures that the attitude and spirit of an armorbearer is found throughout the pages of the New Covenant.

Here are some references to help you discover and study for yourself the proper attitude and character of a New Testament armorbearer: Matt. 18:1-4; John 15:13; Eph. 6:5,6; Phil. 2:3-9; 1 Thess. 5:12,13; 1 Pet. 5:5; 2:20.

5

The Cry of God's Leaders

"Oh, God! Send me a Joshua!"

Now we all know that Joshua was never referred to in the Bible as Moses' armorbearer, but he was called Moses' minister in Joshua 1:1. The verb form of the word *minister* means: to attend, to contribute to, to minister to, to wait on, and to serve. From this definition we see that Joshua's duty was to wait on Moses, to contribute to his success, and to serve him in everything that he did. Had Moses had an armorbearer, it would have been Joshua because of their relationship.

Today apostles, prophets, evangelists, pastors and teachers all across our land are crying out for a man like Joshua to come to their aid. But my question to them is: Are you willing to be a Moses to your Joshua? Now that puts the shoe on the other foot.

What about you? Moses was willing to invest his anointing, and his whole life, into Joshua. He was willing to relinquish control and allow Joshua to take the people on into the Promised Land, even though Moses had personally shepherded the people for forty years in the wilderness. He knew that the children of Israel belonged to God, not to him. He obeyed God when the voice came saying, "Now Joshua will be the one to bring them into the land which I have promised to give them."

I am not saying that this is the situation in your ministry, but I would like for you to see, first of all, that *it's not your ministry,* it's God's.

God placed the vision in you. He birthed it in your spirit. When God starts something, He finishes it. The work God has begun will continue long after you — if you are willing to put yourself into other people, without fear of giving them the authority they need to help you. You can tell how good a leader is by the quality of people following after him.

Here is a list of the basic things to look for, and to do, when seeking a Joshua for your own ministry:

1. Pray for God's divinely-appointed people to come your way.

This is always priority number one.

Ask God to send you quality people to carry your vision forward. The people whom God sends you may be your own personal family, or they may not be.

I once heard a minister say, "I would never let anybody but a member of the family run my ministry." That's a very strong statement, and totally *unscriptural.* The unity between a leader and his staff is in the spirit and not by blood.

God raised up Joshua, not one of Moses' children. God raised up David and elected him to be king, and not Jonathan, who was legal heir to the throne. God told Elijah to go and anoint Elisha as his successor, not one of Elijah's own family members. God anointed Samuel to be priest, not the sons of Eli. In fact, Hophni and Phineas, Eli's sons, were full of evil and wickedness. (1 Sam. 2:22-25.)

Now I will say that God may raise up your son or daughter to carry on your vision, but He could send someone else. The key is for you to do the will of God for your ministry no matter who He may choose to help and succeed you.

Whatever kind of people you need, ask God for them. He will send you an associate, a music director, a head usher, or whatever you may need or desire. You just need to petition Him, and start thanking Him for answering your prayer.

2. Be willing to invest yourself in the lives of your helpers.

Some leaders wonder why they have problems with their staff. Many times the reason is because they have never invested themselves in their associates.

In the Old Testament, the Lord spoke to Moses about those who had been chosen to assist him in leading the children of Israel:

> **And I will come down and talk with thee there: and I will take of the spirit which is upon thee, and will put it upon them; and they shall bear the burden of the people with thee, that thou bear it not thyself alone.**
>
> **Numbers 11:17**

At this time God took the spirit that He had put upon Moses and placed it upon the seventy elders. This was for these elders to function and minister to the people with the same love and anointing with which Moses operated. This was accomplished when Moses laid his hands on his associates, thus imparting the spirit to them.

Where would we be today had Jesus not invested Himself in the disciples? What would have happened if His attitude had been, "I am the leader here, and I don't have time to waste on you weak, faithless disciples"? This kind of attitude has been evident in some leaders, and it is of the devil, not of God. The Lord has not called any of us to control the lives of other people, but to be an example to the flock.

3. Delegate authority.

God desires to send you quality people who can flow with you. But do not be afraid to let them fully express their God-given creativity. Sometimes leaders live in fear that they are losing control because others are beginning to grasp the vision and "run with it."

Do not stifle the enthusiasm, anointing, wisdom and ability of your staff. A smart leader knows how to direct the talents and abilities of his people. You must provide opportunities for your staff members to develop, minister and release their latent creativity. This applies especially to armorbearers who have proven themselves faithful to bless you and help you minister to the people.

If you are going to give anyone responsibility in any area, then be big enough to give him the authority he needs to carry out that responsibility.

An official from Washington, D.C., shared how he had a real problem with authority. He liked the feeling of power it gave him. After becoming a Christian and being called to the pastorate, he said that it was still a struggle for him to delegate authority. In order to break this spirit, he shared how he began to "sow" authority in others.

You will find that, with God, the more you give away, the more God will give back to you.

4. *Look for the spirit of an armorbearer in people.*

Here is a checklist for determining if the people who come your way have the qualifications to become armorbearers:

A. Do they have a disciplined prayer life?

B. Are they faithful to the church?

C. Is their family intact?

D. Are they tithers?

E. Are you at ease in their presence?

F. Are they at ease in your presence?

G. Are they interested in people of all types and races?

H. Do they possess a strong and steady will?

I. Do they avoid murmuring and complaining?

J. Are they optimistic?

K. Do they submit to authority?

L. Are they good listeners?

M. Are they disciplined mentally and physically?

N. Are they loyal?

As you ask and answer these questions about others, always remember to ask *yourself* this important question: *What good is a general without an army to follow him?*

6

How to Develop the Spirit
of an Armorbearer

Every child of God, from leaders on down, needs to develop the character of an armorbearer. I believe that, right now in the Body of Christ, we need teaching on the development of the *character of Christ*. We have learned a lot about faith, prosperity and intercession, but I feel we have got to place more emphasis on character development. God's power is hindered because of our lust for power, money and sex. These things are currently destroying ministries around the world.

I would like to share some steps which I believe will be beneficial to follow in your effort to develop the spirit of a true God-called armorbearer.

Steps to the Development
of the Spirit of an Armorbearer

Step 1. Free yourself from pride. (James 4:6.)

Evidences of pride are:

A. An independent spirit (refusal to look to God or others for help).

B. A failure to admit mistakes.

C. A lack of a teachable spirit.

D. A rebellious attitude toward those in authority.

E. A proud countenance.

F. Self-centered conversation.

G. Intolerance toward the mistakes of others.

H. A bossy attitude.

Step 2: Free yourself from anger. (Prov. 16:32.)

Evidences of anger are:

A. Temper tantrums (at any age).

B. An angry reaction to supposed injustice.

C. Expressed frustration over unchangeable circumstances.

D. Grumbling, murmuring and complaining.

E. Extreme sensitivity and touchiness.

Step 3: Free yourself from immorality. (2 Cor. 7:1.)

Evidences of a spirit of impurity are:

A. Sensual conversation.

B. The reading of impure materials.

C. An impure attitude and improper actions toward members of the opposite sex.

D. A desire to listen to sensual music.

E. Sensual dress or appearance.

F. Carnal curiosity.

Step 4: Free yourself from bitterness. (Heb. 12:15.)

Evidences of a spirit of bitterness are:

A. Sarcastic and critical talk.

B. An inability to trust people.

C. Frequent illness.

D. Self-pity.

E. A sad countenance.

These are all areas in which we need to judge ourselves in order to break Satan's power in our life, to be pleasing to God, and to be the light of the world. This will be accomplished as we lead a life above reproach, giving ourselves totally and freely one for another.

We are God's armorbearers. We are to carry the shield for one another, joining our faith together. If we will do that, we will truly become *God's Great Army.* We will go forth to conquer in the power of the Holy Spirit.

Fields White Unto Harvest

We need each other in order to fulfill God's call on our lives. As we look at what the Lord is doing in Eastern Europe at the time of this writing, we see that now is the time for us in the Church of Jesus Christ to come into "the unity of the faith." (Eph. 4:13.)

I was blessed to be in Austria at the beginning of the mass exodus of East Germans into West Germany when that nation's Communist government lessened travel restrictions to the free world. It was beautiful to see how God had opened the Iron Curtain after all those years. I have never seen people so hungry for freedom as those people were. And thousands of them were also hungry for *God.*

For the first time in over forty years, there is some measure of freedom of religion in many areas of Eastern Europe. The Church must take advantage of the doors which have been so miraculously opened to the spread of the Gospel.

Several years ago my wife and I were in Hungary. When we got ready to minister at a local church, we had to walk out of the hotel and down to the street to make sure we were not being followed. Then we hurried a few blocks to a certain place where the pastor had arranged to pick us up. From there we secretly drove out to a farm house where we preached in an underground church. Now it seems that situation is changing.

I saw on television the opening of the border of Hungary. I watched as the barbwire was being taken down and rolled up. Now visitors can buy a piece of wire with an inscription on it which says: "A part of the Iron Curtain."

I wept as I thought: "If there was ever a time for us to get Bibles into that area, it's now."

God is saying to the Church, "Here is your opportunity."

Billy Graham was in Hungary during the month of August 1989. Over 120,000 people gathered in a stadium to hear him preach the Gospel. So many were saved, it was impossible to get literature to all of them individually, so it was taken and just thrown to the spiritually starved crowds. The ushers believed God that the literature would get to the ones who wanted and needed it most.

Can you see what God is doing in the earth? This move of the Holy Spirit is far greater than the charismatic movement. It's greater than the Baptist church, or the Assemblies of God, or any other single denomination or church group on earth. We Christians must link up together in a joint effort. We must come to understand our anointing, our authority, our assignment, and then begin to flow with each other and God's Spirit.

Vision in a Field

In 1977, while my wife and I were attending school, I didn't have any idea what God had for my life, so I began to seek the Lord. We lived in an apartment building which was located right beside a huge field. Every day, I would get up early in the morning and walk up and down that field, praying and seeking God's direction for my life. I didn't know anybody to help me, and I couldn't figure out how God was going to get me into the ministry.

One day as I was walking up and down that field, I looked toward some high weeds. Suddenly I saw faces of all kinds, shapes and colors: white faces, yellow faces, red faces, black faces. They were all over those weeds. As I gazed at that startling scene, suddenly the anointing of the Lord came upon me and I began to preach. I preached my heart out. I think I must have delivered the best sermon I have ever preached.

When I had finished, I gave an altar call, and people got saved, healed and delivered. A great revival took place right out in that empty field about six o'clock in the morning.

What had happened was that God had impregnated my spirit with a dream, a vision. From that time on, I knew I was going to carry the Gospel to the nations. I didn't have any idea how God was going to bring that vision to reality; I just knew that somehow He would.

My wife and I went on to graduate from school. Then we attended and graduated from Rhema Bible Training Center in Tulsa, Oklahoma. After our Bible studies, God supernaturally brought us to Little Rock, Arkansas, where we became associated with Agape Church.

In 1982, I began to see my vision come to pass. I started to travel overseas, making contact with people who were doing great things for God. That fall, we opened the Agape School for World Evangelism. My dream was becoming reality.

It was during this time that the Lord spoke to me from 1 Samuel 16:21. He told me to get my priorities into proper order. I learned that I was to be my pastor's armorbearer and to stand with him to fulfill the vision God had placed in his heart.

The Anointing of an Armorbearer

In order to develop the true spirit of an armorbearer, the first step is to understand our anointing. We have noted that an armorbearer is anointed to carry another man's shield into battle. His call and duty is to lay down his life for someone else.

In 2 Kings 3:11 we read: **But Jehoshaphat said, Is there not here a prophet of the Lord, that we may inquire of the Lord by him? And one of the king of Israel's servants answered and said, Here is Elisha the son of Shaphat, which poured water on the hands of Elijah.**

I believe that right now there are people who have been faithful to "pour water on the hands of their Elijah." You mark it down, the anointing of God is coming upon them. God is raising up all kinds of people, and the ones He is looking for are those who have shown themselves to be loyal servants, anointed as armorbearers.

The Word of the Lord may be with you, as it was with Elisha, because God looks at the heart. He looked at Elisha's heart, and the Word of the Lord was with him.

The Mantle of a Prophet

I wonder, if Elijah were alive today, how many people would be standing in line wanting to receive his mantle? I have a feeling Elijah would be very rough with them. I believe he would tell them, "Get your own mantle!"

Every true believer has his own mantle of anointing. We do not need to covet another man's mantle or anointing.

Elisha remained faithful to Elijah under all kinds of different circumstances. Historians tell us that Elisha served Elijah for about fifteen to twenty years. By this we know that Elisha heard everything that Elijah said, and saw everything he did, whether good or bad.

When King Ahab sent soldiers after Elijah, he was sitting on a hill. Elijah cried out to the captain of the guard, **...If I be a man of God, then let fire come down from heaven, and consume thee and thy fifty...**(2 Kings 1:10). The fire fell, and fifty men died, leaving fifty horses to go running back to town with empty saddles.

How would you have responded if you had been Elijah's associate at this time? You would have thought to yourself, "Boy, am I glad I'm on his side!" You would have been proud to tell everyone, "I work for Elijah."

Recognizing the Human Side of Leaders

In 1 Kings 18:17-40, we see another time that fire came down from heaven at Elijah's request. This time it was to consume a sacrifice offered to the Lord. We all remember the story of the famous contest on Mount Carmel between Elijah and the heathen prophets to prove which was the true God: Jehovah or Baal. After the Lord had sent fire from heaven to consume the sacrifice, His prophet, Elijah, took a sword and slew the four hundred prophets of Baal.

Following an experience like that, you would think that this man would not be afraid of anything. But we read that when the wicked Queen Jezebel sent a message threatening the life of Elijah, he became frightened and fled into the wilderness. (2 Kings 19:1-4.)

How do you respond when your leader reacts in fear, when you discover that he is human just as you are? As Elijah's associate, what would you have said to him? You would probably have stood and shouted to him as he ran, "Oh man of spirit and power, come back!" Here is an important question. Have you seen your leader fall? Have you seen him make a great mistake and even get into sin? What's your reaction? Are you ready to leave and find some other place of employment, or are you willing to help, support and see him restored? Here is where we really find out what we are made of. If there is a true attitude of repentance, a faithful man will stand with his leader. Proverbs 11:13 says, **A talebearer revealeth secrets: but he that is of a faithful spirit concealeth the matter.** A true armorbearer knows how to control his tongue in public, but how to speak boldly in prayer.

Elisha remained faithful to Elijah, and because of this faithfulness, when the time came for Elijah to leave this earth, Elisha could ask for a double portion of his anointing. (2 Kings 2:9.) Elijah knew the heart of the young man who had served him so well. He told Elisha that if he saw him when he left the earth, then his request would be granted. (v. 10.) When Elijah departed, Elisha was there to watch him being taken up into heaven in a fiery chariot. (v. 11.) Elijah's mantle fell from his shoulders at the feet of Elisha. It was then, at that time, that the anointing doubled.

In these last days, I expect to see a similar doubling, or even a tripling, of God's anointing upon His people. But it will come upon those who have been faithful to their Elijah. Whether you see your leader do great things, or make great mistakes, you must still remain faithful to him.

In Revelation 4:7, we see the four faces of Jesus:

And the first beast was like a lion, and the second beast like a calf, and the third beast had a face as a man, and the fourth was like a flying eagle.

A lion, a calf, a man and an eagle. We see Jesus as a lion in dealing with the devil and sin. We see Him as a calf as He came to serve humanity. We see Him as a man as He held the little children and blessed them. And we see Him as an eagle as He prayed, preached and healed the people.

In every leader you will see a lion, when it comes to dealing with a problem; a calf, when it comes to serving people; a man, when it comes to tending the sheep; and as an eagle, when it comes to standing up to minister the Word of the Lord. But you will also see your leader as a man when he is hurt and wounded.

Most people only see their leader as an eagle, but you will see your leader in all four faces. You will see him when he is less than full of faith and power, when he says something or does something that may offend you, when things are tight financially and you have to cut back the budget of your department.

It is easy to respect your pastor when he is functioning as an eagle under God's anointing. But you must also respect him when times are hard and he is operating more as a man. Respect is due the leader no matter how he may appear or feel.

Some people have the mistaken idea that those who work in the ministry sit around all day, praying in tongues and prophesying to one another. The ministry, however, is *work, work* and more *work*. It requires an ability to work with other people without giving or taking offense. True armorbearing is the ability to see the human side of our leaders and still maintain respect for them.

Recognizing the Right of Divine Authority

The second area that we must come to understand in order to be true armorbearers is the right of divine authority. We must know, recognize and yield to God's authority in our lives. We have to pray daily, "Father, not my will, but Thine be done." We have to be determined in our hearts to stay in God's will regardless of the cost or consequences.

When we look at Jesus, we might think that because He was the Son of God He had no problem at all in fulfilling God's will for His life. Let's look at Hebrews 5:7,8 to see if this is true:

> **Who in the days of his flesh, when he had offered up prayers and supplications with *strong crying* and *tears* unto him that was able to save him from death, and was heard in that he feared;**
>
> **Though he were a Son, yet learned he obedience by the things which he suffered.**

We see Jesus in "strong crying and tears" before the Father, yet choosing to remain in God's will for His life and praying to fulfill the divine call that was upon Him.

Whatever it takes, whether you are happy or hurting, make a firm commitment in your heart to fulfill God's plan for your life.

Several years ago the Lord said something to me that has helped me during hard times. He said: "Keep your eyes on the resurrection, and you can endure the cross." The cross is not a burden; it's the call of God on our lives. If it is God's will for you to stay in one place for the rest of your life in order to give yourself to and for someone else, then let God's will be done.

Giving Birth to God's Will

One day I was thinking of what God has placed in my heart to do for Him. I have a God-ordained desire to see churches and Bible schools raised up in all nations around the world. I asked the Lord one time, "Father, how is this vision going to ever come into reality?"

He said to me: "Son, you are going to have to bring it forth by *intimacy, pregnancy, travail,* and *birth.*"

Spiritual birth takes place the same way that natural birth occurs. In order to bring forth in the spiritual realm, we have to get intimate with God. From

71

that intimacy comes pregnancy. From pregnancy will eventually come travail, and then, finally, birth.

We must give birth to the fulfillment of God's will in our lives. The fulfillment of our God-given vision will not drop down on us out of the sky. We must draw nigh to God, and then He will draw nigh to us. (James 4:8.)

Some of the most miserable people in this world are women who are are pregnant and overdue. Likewise, some of the most miserable Christians in the world are those who are "pregnant" with a vision from God, and yet have not been able to give birth to that vision. But intimacy with God must come first, before there can ever be a pregnancy.

I believe that today the Holy Spirit is speaking the words of Hosea 10:12 to the Body of Christ: **Sow to yourselves in righteousness, reap in mercy; break up your fallow ground:** *for it is time to seek the Lord,* **till he come and rain righteousness upon you.**

To become intimate with the Lord, we must seek Him with our whole heart.

Once we have developed an intimate relationship with God, we will get pregnant with a dream or a vision which has been planted in us by the Lord. Then we must take that vision which has been supernaturally planted in us by God and begin to nurture it, causing to it to grow and develop. Sooner or later it will lead to godly travail, without which there can be no birth. That travail is our intercession.

Isaiah 40:3 speaks of: **The voice of him that crieth in the wilderness, Prepare ye the way of the Lord, make straight in the desert a highway for our God.**

John the Baptist was the forerunner of Jesus. He prepared the way for Jesus' first coming. You and I are preparing the way for the Lord's second coming.

One day the Lord revealed Isaiah 40:3 to me in this way: "The voice of him that crieth in Little Rock, Arkansas, prepare ye the way of the Lord, make straight in Little Rock a highway for our God."

Intercession is like building a highway for the Lord. We have to do the the work first, and then God will send His glory. If we will be patient and faithful, if we will follow the process of intimacy, pregnancy, travail and birth, we will see the fulfillment of our heavenly dream and vision.

Following God's Predetermined Course

...being predestinated according to the purpose of him who worketh all things after the counsel of his own will.

Ephesians 1:11

The word translated **predestinated** in this verse means "predetermined." God has a predetermined, predesigned course for everyone of us. That course was set before we were ever born into this earth.

The Lord has said to each of us: **Before I formed thee in the belly I knew thee...**(Jer. 1:5.) God knew you and me before the foundation of the world, and He set an individual course for each of us to follow. Now it is up to you and me to discover God's course for us and to follow that course so that we may give spiritual birth to the dream and vision He has had in mind for us from before the creation of the world.

I know that, at this time, I am called to be an armorbearer to my pastor. And because I am determined to stay in God's will, every promise in God's Word can be fulfilled in my life.

The Apostle Paul said, **I have fought a good fight, I have finished my course...**(2 Tim. 4:7). Paul fought to stay on course, and he made it. He finished the course laid out for him by God.

Discover what your course is, and then stay with it and never give up until you have reached your God-ordained destination and goal.

Understanding Our Assignment and Appreciating Our Gifts

The last important step we need to take is to learn and understand our God-given assignment. The fulfillment of that assignment is dependent upon the proper use of the divine gifts which have been bestowed upon us.

Every year my family gets together on Christmas Eve. Because my family is so large, prior to Christmas we draw names to see who we will buy presents for. One Christmas, while handing out the gifts, I noticed that my twin brother had received two presents. His name had accidentally been placed on two different gifts. When I opened my present, I was disappointed in what I got. I looked at my twin brother and he was laughing because he had received two nice gifts. Seeing my disappointed expression, my wife came over to console me.

"Don't worry, Terry," she said, "when we get back home, we will exchange it for something you like better."

Now the very same thing happens in the Body of Christ. We open the gifts God has given us, and we run to someone else to see what he got. Then we hurry to another to see what gift he has received. When we look at our gift from the Lord, we are unhappy with it and immediately think to ourselves, "I know what I'll do; I'll swap it for something I like better."

This is why there are so many people running around in church circles today claiming to be an apostle or a prophet or a teacher. Many times what they are really doing is "gift swapping," because they do not like the spiritual gift which God has bestowed upon them.

We must know in our hearts that we had absolutely nothing to do with choosing the gifts that God has placed inside of each of us. He bestows gifts according to His will, and it is up to us to receive those gifts and allow the Lord to add to us more gifts "as He wills." (1 Cor. 12:11.)

> But now hath God set the members every one of
> them in the body, as it hath pleased him.
> 1 Corinthians 12:18

As we are faithful in the small things, God will make us rulers over many. (Matt. 25:21.) As we stay with the assignment and the gifts God has given each of us, He will bring our gift before great men.

I remember one day while attending Bible school, I saw a fellow I knew come into class all dressed up. This was unusual because he generally wore jeans. When I asked him why he was so dressed up, he answered, "Because all the 'big shots' from the denominational headquarters are coming to school today; just stick with me and I'll introduce you to the really big ones."

I got so mad I went to my room and told the Lord that if that was how the ministry works, then He could count me out of it. The Lord said so clearly to me that day, "Son, don't you realize that you have already been introduced to the Big One"?

That's right. They don't come any "bigger" than God. Stay with your individual assignment, and in due time the Lord will exalt you.

I went through a time when I saw God begin to do many great things in my life. It was a time of the manifestation and fulfillment of many dreams and visions. During this period, I started experiencing more problems and having more frequent confrontations than ever before in my life. As director of our Bible and mission school, I felt like a fireman. As soon as one "blaze" was extinguished, another would crop up somewhere else. It seemed as if everything I did was wrong.

Now on the one hand, God was doing great things, but on the other hand I felt run down and discouraged. At this time I thought to myself, "I will just let my wife (who is the administrator of the school) start doing more; I'll go to the mission field where the work is fun and I can just send back picture postcards."

Now my mind was made up to do that until, while in prayer, I saw in my spirit a vision of David being anointed by Samuel. I saw the oil running down his head as he was anointed king of Israel. At that time, the Lord asked me this question: "What did David do after he was anointed king?"

I thought for a moment and answered, "He went back to tending his father's sheep in the field."

The Lord spoke to me: "Had David gone out looking for a giant to kill at this time, the lion and the bear would have eaten his flock. That school is your flock, so you had better see to it."

"Yes, Sir," I said, "I see that very clearly."

Whether we are a pastor, an associate pastor, a music director or a layman, each of us has a flock. That flock belongs to us individually, and God expects us to tend it. David's flock was his assignment from God, and he knew that, although he had been anointed to be king of Israel, his first priority right at the moment was to continue to tend to his first assignment.

You see, the giants will come. But, if you will stay with your assignment, when the time comes you will meet and conquer your giant just as David met and overcame his. Like David, you will be exalted, *after* you have first proven yourself faithful.

I knew personally that if I did not take the time to put myself into the students under my care, I could not expect them to flow with me once they had reached the mission field.

You may look at your current condition and position and wonder how God could ever use you. You may think to yourself: "I am not the person in charge, so I have to stay submitted to other people. How will I ever get to fulfill my own dream and vision?" Be at peace and know that God's Word is not written for leaders only. It is written for the Body of Christ, and that includes you — right where you are today.

The Mission of the Church in the Last Days

Recently I was in Austria and was talking with a national pastor. He shared with me something that blessed me greatly.

In 1987, when I was in that country, I was scheduled to lead a Bible conference. I struggled within myself as to what to teach. I rose up early the day before the conference and said to the Lord, "Father, what do You want me to teach?" I had not consulted with Him about His direction.

The Lord said, "Preach on the pattern of the New Testament church."

I began reading through the book of Acts to discover what that pattern was. The theme of all the messages I received was: "If Austria is going to be won to God, it must be done through the local church."

I realized then that God was saying, "Today is the day of the local church in Austria." I believe that is true of the whole world.

This Austrian pastor shared with me how as a result of that one conference, four local churches had been started in four different areas. I was so blessed and moved in my heart that God had used me to affect a nation. It had happened because I was obedient and taught what He wanted taught.

In 1989, we opened the first Full-Gospel Bible school in the history of that European nation. I have found God to be so faithful to us as we determine to *walk in our anointing,* to *stay in submission to His divine authority,* and to *fulfill our God-ordained assignment.* It takes an understanding of all these areas in order to be an armorbearer.

Ours could very well be the generation that rises to meet Jesus in the air. It is time for us to re-evaluate our lives, and our ministries, to make sure that we are where we need to be and doing what we need to be doing. Satan does not mind our building our dreams and visions, as long as he is the head contractor. If what we are doing is not of the Spirit and directed by Him, any edifice we erect is going to fall. (Ps. 127:1.) Satan will allow us to build, making sure that we smear God's name all over our own dreams and visions, so that when they fail it will appear that God has failed.

When we set out to build the Kingdom, we must be sure that God is one hundred percent in and behind what we are doing.

The spirit of an armorbearer is the Spirit of Christ. This is the day we see that God's children should take up the shields of others and be willing to carry them forth into battle. We have an overall vision and mandate from God to reach our generation. This can be accomplished when we develop the spirit of an armorbearer and truly begin to give of ourselves.

The armorbearers of today will be the leaders of tomorrow.

To contact Terry Nance
for a complete list of tapes and materials,
write:

Terry Nance
Agape Church
P.O. Box 22007
Little Rock, Arkansas 72221

*Please include your prayer requests
and comments when you write.*

Additional copies of
God's Armorbearer
are available from your local bookstore,
or from:

Harrison House
P.O. Box 35035
Tulsa, OK 74153